T0149396

# JUST A HEARTBEAT AWAY

*The silver barrier*

MIKE PAPPAS

## JUST A HEARTBEAT AWAY
## THE SILVER BARRIER

*iUniverse books may be ordered through booksellers or by contacting:*

*iUniverse*
*1663 Liberty Drive*
*Bloomington, IN 47403*
*www.iuniverse.com*
*1-800-Authors (1-800-288-4677)*

*Because of the dynamic nature of the Internet, any web addresses or links contained in this book may have changed since publication and may no longer be valid. The views expressed in this work are solely those of the author and do not necessarily reflect the views of the publisher, and the publisher hereby disclaims any responsibility for them.*

*Any people depicted in stock imagery provided by Getty Images are models, and such images are being used for illustrative purposes only. Certain stock imagery © Getty Images.*

*ISBN: 978-1-5320-8948-0 (sc)*
*ISBN: 978-1-5320-8949-7 (e)*

*Print information available on the last page.*

*iUniverse rev. date: 12/12/2019*

# CONTENTS

# ACKNOWLEDGMENTS

I dedicate this book to all the EMS's, doctors, nurses, nurses' aides and therapist who contributed to my recovery.

# "INTRODUCTION"

Before you read my story let me introduce myself my name is Mike Pappas and I was born and raised in New York City in 1940 and lived with my parents and four siblings. Our parents immigrated from Greece in the mid-1930s. We were raised at a time when things were simple and basic, even though the times were tough. Our father had passed away when we were still young; I was just nine years old. My mother did a remarkable job raising us to what we are today.

At that time, I thought I was eating healthy. My mother most of the time would cook healthy vegetable meals especially during the Lenten season. When it came to Sundays and holidays things were a lot different, she would cook roasts and mostly red meats and it was rare. Which unfortunately grew on me; I got to love red meat especially steaks and of course they were rare.

I was drafted into the Army in 1962 and spent 13 months in Korea. I was a victim of a Dear John. As it turned out I later met the love of my life Marsha, in which she gave me three great sons Charles, John and Michael and could not want anything more. We were blessed with a grandson Ethan in Florida. This is our 2nd grandchild, we had sadly lost our first grandson Noah a couple years earlier at birth.

I consider myself to have been in good health growing up and into my adult life. It was not until I reached my early sixty's when things started to happen. First, I was diagnosed with colon cancer and then a few years later prostate cancer. I had most of my colon removed and had a seed implant in my prostate. I was fortunate to have caught them in the early stages.

What is life all about; I guess we take it for granted not knowing what tomorrow might bring. That old saying "live every day to its fullest."

After retiring I made it a point not to let silly things bother me. Since I retired, my wife Marsha and I would go to Myrtle Beach during the winter and fall season. We were getting ready for a fall get-away week of relaxation, something we always look forward to and always felt good to get away, it was a change of pace from the everyday routine.

# "UNEXPECTED"

I will never forget that morning we were packed up and ready to take our fall vacation and make an extra stop to see our grandson Ethan. I would every six months see my doctors without failure. I felt good knowing that I had just seen all my doctors, had blood work an EKG and a nuclear stress test done, and everything was normal.

We left our house about 4:30am still dark and a light rain to catch our flight. We found leaving from Atlantic City airport was always more convenient even though it was a longer ride. Everything was as usual, park the car grabbed our luggage and started walking to the terminal, feeling fine. We retrieve our label from the kiosk for our luggage and from there we went online to check our luggage. Waiting patiently to be called I started feeling a little lightheaded. Before I could even utter a word, it was lights out.

I was unresponsive and basic life support was administered, followed by AED, which advised shock treatment not once but twice I then returned to spontaneous circulation. I was then put into an ambulance, apparently had a V-fib arrest procedure done and witnessed in the ambulance. They had to cut my clothing off to perform the procedure, something we did not know until the day I was leaving the hospital when I went to put my clothing on. All my belongings were given to my wife Marsha, I was then taken to the emergency room at Atlantic City care regional hospital.

The next thing I remember was waking up, feeling strange and trying to focus on my surroundings; it was a blur and felt this tube down my throat, and all these different wires and I V's connected to my body. Still not realizing where I was. I slowly started to see images but was not able to communicate except with my hands; everything was still a blur but could hear voices. I even try to move but couldn't; it felt like I was in the twilight zone.

When I fully regained consciousness, I could hear someone saying he is moving and was told to squeeze his hand and wiggle my toes; in which I was able to do. After a few seconds or maybe it was a minute I could see all kinds of people mostly wearing white all around me. I was confused not truly realizing what had happen, was I dreaming?

I realized it was no dream; but in a hospital. I then saw my wife and sons Charles and Michael asking me "how I felt." Being I could not talk I gave them a thumbs down. Shortly later my son John flew in from Florida. I could just imagine what they were thinking seeing me in this condition.

I wanted so badly to pull the tube from my mouth it was that irritable. They could see me trying to pull it out of my mouth and the nurse said, "it will be removed shortly." A short time later they remove the tube from my throat, it was only in a short time, but it felt like hours. I then threw up it was that irritable; I was told it was to get my circulation back to normal. I was still in a state of confusion and did not say much.

Once I was done with this procedure, they started doing all kinds of test from a brain scan, MRI's to x-rays, and blood work which took almost the whole day. They were having a hard time trying to draw blood, my veins would hide, giving the nurses a difficult time. After several attempts they finally caught a vein. The head nurse had request that they would put a port on my neck so they could draw blood when needed which she said would be almost every day. So, they schedule the procedure which would be done if I would require surgery.

Later the doctor came into the room and said I have all the test results, the brain scan showed nothing and I said, "I could have told you that," he chuckled and said, "it's good to see you have a good sense of humor after what you went thru." He went on and said all other tests came out normal. Some of my blood work was a little out of range, but medication will be able to correct that.

From the time I awaken I had no pain as if nothing happened. Little by little I was getting to realize my situation. It's amazing what goes thru one's mind and I could not help thinking back years earlier when I was told that my body made its own collateral bypass. Something rare with many, what they thought was a heart attack was my body making its own bypass.

# III

# "THE SILVER BARRIER"

his had to be a real trauma for Marsha to witness this mishap, with all the commotion she forgot our luggage. She later had to retreat our luggage from the airport; in which our son John took her. While she was claiming the luggage, John spoke with a few of the employees and one of them remembered the incident and told him exactly what she saw. She had a clear view and said, "he was standing and suddenly started to lean and then fell backwards hitting the barrier pole that seemed to break his fall, and most likely avoided any possibly of a head injury or other trauma."

When I got back my composure, I asked them what happen, all I could remember was being on line at the airport to check our luggage then waking up here in the hospital, and even then, I was confused where I was or even remember anything in between.

When they told me, what happened I think back and was very fortunate that it occurred at the airport in Atlantic City; just imagining being on the airplane or even driving. I'm thinking to myself thank God that barrier was there. They say timing is everything, and after this I'll agree to that.

I had to remind them about the car, and they assured me not to worry, later they got our car from the airport. In all the years we flew we never purchased flight insurance. Marsha suggested to purchase some, I always said," what could happen." So being the price was reasonable I did. It was like she anticipated something, call it coincidental!

Now it was the waiting game, I had no idea what they were going to do next. All crazy things were going thru my mind. I was wondering how this all came about. One thing about being in a hospital you have all the time to think about everything!

# "HEART NEWS"

O ne of the cardiologists came into the room to explain the next procedure they were going to perform. He went into detail and explained the procedure was a catherization to check blood flow to and from my heart to determine what caused my situation.

Hearing this, I must admit I was a nervous wreck and even scared to hear what they will discover, but it had to be done. I had one done about twelve years earlier.

Before he did the procedure, he gave me a light sedation, I could hear him talking while he was doing the procedure. It did not take long, but I could sense the results were serious.

Later when I went back to my room, he told us what he found.  I developed paroxysmal atrial fibrillation and converted back to sinus rhythm on amiodarone.  In laymen's terms, my heart stop beating due to an irregular heart rate that commonly causes poor blood flow.  He also said, "right now it looks like a triple by-pass and hopefully we won't find any other problems." Three of my arteries were 90% blocked two of them were the collateral by-pass my body had made years earlier.  This all had to contributed to my mishap.

The first thing that came to mind was the stress test.  Why did it not show up I was totally confused? What is the purpose of taking the test; if it did not show the problem?

After the results were given to us, the surgeon came to tell us what he was going to do in detail.  I then ask him about the stress test, his remark was it is only 90% accurate, and the facts are because all three of the arteries were at the same degree it would not show any change.

Call me thick headed I was still not satisfied with his answer; I just felt how many people are walking around not knowing this.  "The good news was my heart suffered no damage."

The surgeon asked me and my family if we wanted the surgery done here or go to another hospital.  He suggested having it done here, it was our choice, "talk it over".

My son Michael did some research and found out they had a good track record, on this kind of surgery, especially our surgeon. Being they knew my history and all the testing was done here; besides we had no other hospital in mind we decided to have it done here.

Because this happened on a Wednesday, they wanted to wait a few days for my heart to heal from the trauma it had endured. Now that meant the earliest would be Monday. This had to be the longest few days I had to wait.

One can imagine what was on my mind all these days of waiting. I was assured the surgeon had done hundreds, if not thousands of this type of operation.

They later came into my room and were going to put the port in my neck so they could draw blood when needed. The nurse had this huge needle it looked like a spear to me. I could feel her putting the needle in an artery, and blood was starting to flow. So, no more jabbing needles in my arm, in a way it was going to be better all-around.

Being this mishap occurred far from home I was not expecting any visitors. My family was with me every day even after the surgery was completed. The phone did not stop ringing when the word got out, wishing me good luck and a speedy recovery.

One would think with all the testing and lab work I had just endured they still wanted to do more test before my surgery. With all I have been thru any other testing was just another formality in my eyes.

The day before my surgery I was put on a liquid diet, just thinking about the surgery I had no real appetite.

The night before the surgery just after my family left, I was having flash backs from when I was a kid to the present. I sat in the lounge chair most of the night trying not to think about tomorrow. Looking at the clock which did not seem to move, I was ready to throw a towel over it. One of the nurses came in about 2am and we spoke a little and later help me get into bed. I was trying to sleep but I had too much on my mind.

# "A NEW BEGINNING"

The big day arrived, and I was awakened even though I never did sleep just thinking about the surgery. First a nurse came and shaved my chest down to my legs and every place in between, then she washes me down; I looked like a seal. Another nurse came in and gave me a red heart shaped pillow, she explained the use of the pillow "it will be your best friend." Then she helps me remove my hospital gown and put on this different type of gown. Both nurses wish me good luck.

Two nurses' aides came, and they ask me my name and date of birth and bought in a moveable bed. While they were taking me to the operating room all crazy things were going thru my head.

The operating room looked like Frankenstein's laboratory only modern. They moved me again onto another bed where they were going to do the surgery. I never saw so many nurses in one place at one time except maybe in the cafeteria. It felt like I was back at my old job; the operating room felt like a meat cooler; they place this warm blanket over my body. I asked one of the nurses why it's so cold. She replied, "to keep the bacterium count low and to avoid unnecessary infections."

Again, one of the nurses asked me my name, date of birth. I guess they wanted to be sure they are operating on the correct patient. Then the anesthesiologist explained what he was going to do and what to expect when I came out of surgery. I must admit I was nervous maybe that I won't come out of this.

It's amazing at that moment you think back at the things you did not do. A few minutes later the anesthesiologist started to do his procedure, he says first he would give me an intravenous to relax me. Within minutes I felt like I was on a cloud, then he put a mask over my mouth and nose. I had looked at the clock just before I went under.

# "RECOVERY"

I could hear sounds and voices realizing the surgery was over and trying to focus on my surroundings. What seemed like a few minutes turned out to be over four hours. When I opened my eyes, I recognize one of the nurses from the operating room she asks me "how I felt," I remember telling her "that I am feeling very tired." She said it's the anesthesia is still in your system and by tomorrow I'll be feeling like a new person. You might have some side effect down the road and not to worry because that is normal.

She noticed a swelling and redness on my left wrist and ask me how long I have had that, because it looks nasty. I told her "that's strange, it was not there before my surgery." Like I needed more problems. They had to give me some medication to help with the swelling.

She says your family is waiting to see you. It was good to see them, and it made me feel that much better. Michael noticed my hand and said, "what happened?" "Like I told the nurse it was not there before the surgery." After a short visit they told me "get some rest, and they will see me in my room."

The same two aides moved me to my new room which was ICU; I had my own personal nurses, a male nurse Bob and a female nurse Stephanie who was like an angel they both catered to all my needs.

I was glad I had the room to myself, especially now during my healing. They check my vitals and discovered my blood pressure was running on the high side and they would try to get the proper milligrams needed. The male nurse says you have new plumbing and we need to adjust the medication. After a few days they managed to keep me at a safe zone.

When they were changing the bandages from my leg I noticed where they took the blood vessels to do the surgery," I said it sure looks ugly." I ask the nurse Stephanie about it and she said, "it looks better than others I have seen." That made me feel a little better.

Both nurses also commented on my swelling wrist and said the same thing "it looks nasty." I told them it had to happen while I was in surgery. They check my chart and updated and gave me a stronger medication. The nurse Stephanie placed a warm compress to help control the swelling.

They told me I needed to wear these special stockings, so they fit me with what they call compression

stockings. They covered almost my whole leg to help with my swelling that developed during the time in the hospital. What a job it took to put them on I felt helpless knowing I could do nothing but watch; taking them off was not as bad. I had to wear them all day and before going to bed they removed them.

My sons ask the nurses many questions, hoping to find out more about my surgery and the healing. I would just take one day at a time!

The next day after the anesthesia wore off, I could feel some pain where they cut me and broke my cavity bone to do the surgery. The nurse asks me if I wanted something for the pain and I said a flat no, thank you.

When I looked at my incision, it looked like a zipper; it went down my chest and continue when I had my colon surgery. They told me be sure to keep it dry, to avoid it from getting infected. Another concern to add to my list.

I could not get used to the hospital bed. I would toss and turn knowing I could not sleep on my belly which was how I slept, making it difficult trying to find a convenient sleeping position. Sleeping on a king size bed at home made it feel like I was sleeping on an ironing board. So, I decided and would spend more time in a lounge chair.

# "MY FIRST STEP"

Not wasting any time, they had me out of bed
and just to get out of bed was a big ordeal.
Thanks for my heart-shape pillow, I would
hug it and it took a lot of pressure off my chest. They
wanted to give me a walker, but I refused one, mainly
because I did not want to rely on it. When I started
walking, I found it difficult to walk so I took the I V
roller to help me keep my balance.

After a few times, I no longer needed the I V roller
and would hug my pillow as support. At the beginning I
could hardly walk, just a few steps and I was exhausted.

The nurse saw that I was out of breath and said,
"just take it slow and walk at your own comfortable
pace."

They gave me this device to blow into ten times every hour to get my lugs active and prevent the chance of fluids developing around my lungs. They gave me a starting goal of 750 M I at first, I found it difficult to get to that level. My nurse would scold me when she saw I was not using it as needed.

My pillow was a life-saver even when I had to cough, I hugged it. The nurse was not kidding that the pillow was going to be my best friend, I made sure wherever I went it came with me.

The nurse gave me a list of restrictions; I could not pick up anything that weighed more than five pounds, could not sleep on my belly or could not raise my hands over my head or put them behind me. I say loudly, "oh no how do I wipe myself when I must use the bathroom" My angel nurse said not to worry.

The surgeon and his pretty assistant came in to see how I was doing and check my incision, he said it is healing good and everything went well. He said I'm sure they already told you it's very important to keep the incision dry and clean to avoid any kind of infection for the next 60 days. He explained and confirmed that three of my arteries were 90% block and was very fortunate the way things turned out. Also, it would take anywhere from six to eight weeks for all to heal, and maybe longer before I could do anything active like driving. The reason was the airbags in the car would be dangerous in case they activated, I had to sit in the rear of the car with no exceptions, another restriction to add to my list.

I could sense the surgeon was very compassionate when he spoke. He said, "It will take time and you will be back to your normal self if you stay active and continue your therapy and exercises." He also noticed my left hand and made a comment "how did that happen?" I explain what I felt happened. He said, "be sure they take care of it because it doesn't look good." Instead of getting better It was getting worse.

When everything was going well; my son John went home. The others stayed locally at a hotel in Atlantic City. Mainly because it was a long ride home every day.

The next day my son Michael told me he could not sleep and went down to the casino to play and had won a thousand dollars. I said, "at least something good happened."

After a few days, I told them to go home, that I would be all right. Michael said, "they would stay a little longer." Charles had to go back to work, so he left, it was just my wife and Michael who stayed.

With all the medication I was taking my sugar level was a little elevated. This had occurred years earlier when I was in the hospital before. They suggested taking a pill, I was taking so many medications that I was a little relucted to take it. Just like me, I started taking the medication.

I was on a liquid diet from the day before surgery and they said I should start eating solid foods. I had no appetite and I question them about it, and they said, "it should be alright."

They brought my dinner and the smell alone made me nauseous. The nurse told me to eat because I needed the energy. I took a few bites and no sooner I swallowed my dinner I puke it up and then some. What a mess the nurse had to change the sheets as well as my sleeping gown, and my poor pillow got wet.

So, I had a little set-back, and this went on for a few more days, I could not keep anything down. In my opinion, I think I should have stayed on the liquid diet a few more days. Which of course they did, they ran a test to discover that my stomach was still not ready for solids. I was also thinking maybe that pill I took could have had a roll in my set back.

I was taking so many kinds of medications I was not even sure what I was taking anymore. Just as fast as I started taking that pill for the sugar level, they took me off it. I was thinking about everything that may have played a roll; also remembering what the nurse from the operating room said to me about the aftereffects.

My nurse Stephanie told me this kind of surgery can sometimes effective everything in your system either shuts down or goes into a relax stage. All I could do was take one day at a time.

As the days passed, I started to feel better and getting stronger, so they talk about moving me to a regular room. No sooner they told me an aid came into my room with a wheelchair to move me.

I was going to miss the personal care I received in ICU. But it also felt good knowing that part was behind me. I thank both my nurses for their outstanding attention and care.

I never did find out what really cause my nausea, maybe it was best I did not know.

Like I said I wasn't expecting any visitors, but to my surprise two of John's friends Drew and Mark paid me a visit on different days. It just so happened they were in town on business. Not having many visitors, it always felt good to have company. The doctors and nurses were constantly coming in and out of my room all day even at night, so I never got bored in that respect.

Every morning a nurse would come in at the crack of dawn and attend me, help walk me to the bathroom, weigh me and then give me a hot sponge bath, check my incision and change my bandages. The first few days they would give me a sponge bath and then I started doing it myself, except in places I could not reach. They were spoiling me, when I got home was my wife going to continue where they left off. After a few days, they removed all my bandages so the wounds would heal faster.

Being I was diagnosed with a heart arrhythmia they suggested I should have a defibrillator; they were scheduled to fit me with one. This was minor surgery compared with what I went thru. They explain the purpose of it was in the event it happens again it would jump-start my heart if needed. Plus, a report is sent to my heart doctor when needed or request one.

The defibrillator was going to be placed just below my left shoulder. They took me down to have the procedure done, and I made sure I took my pillow with me. Two nurses got me prepared for the procedure and asked me my name and date of birth. They ask me if I had any questions, so I told them about my nausea.

They pass the information on. The anesthesia's was concerned because of my nausea, he felt because with other dose of anesthesia it could make matters even worse and suggest waiting a few days.

After what I went thru, I agreed, and they took me back to my room. My wife, son Michael, and the nurse were surprised to see me back so soon; I explain to them what happened.

Remembering, I was not permitted to put my hands behind my back, so when it came down to do my thing, I had to rely on the nurse to wipe and clean me. The first time I must admit I felt embarrassed, but after a few times it came naturally. I have to say a nurse is more than just a nurse they do things one would never expect.

One of the hospital therapists came to see me and ask me questions about my recent surgery and my personal history. She explained the importance of therapy, and wanted me to do some walking, because it was important to keep the body moving.

Being I had walk earlier I thought it would not be as hard. I could not believe how tired and exhausted I got just walking a few steps. Again, thank God for my pillow. At the beginning I would make an excuse when they wanted me to walk? That's how tired I got.

I realized if I wanted to get my strength back, I had to walk. So little by little I force myself and started to walk further each day, I must admit I was totally exhausted after each walk. I came to realize; it seems the longer you delay walking the harder it gets. The one nurse said if you think we are pushing you wait until you go to physical therapy.

After constantly being yelled at I got into a routine and found myself blowing into the devise easier. So, when they discover it, they raised my level to 1000 ml.

After several days they were going to try solid foods again, I was a little reluctant at first. So, I order something light hoping that I would not experience what happened earlier. My appetite was coming back with no side effects; little by little I was eating more each day, and before I realized my appetite was back to normal. That made me feel better.

Finally, I was going to have the defibrillator put in; my wife and son Michael were there to give me moral support. Everything went well and within a couple of hours I was back in my room.

I could feel a difference and was not nearly as tired this time compared to my heart surgery. They gave me another restriction I could not raise my left hand for two weeks, just to be sure I did not pull the wire connection to my heart. Otherwise they would have to redo the procedure again, no thanks.

I almost forgot a few times trying to raise my left hand but caught myself. I had the nurse put a sling on my arm to remind me.

At first, I could not feel the defibrillator, then I went to wash up I could see the incision and this bulge just under my shoulder, it looked like a wallet.

An associate with the defibrillator company came the following day to program it. He explained how it worked and what I had to do. Basically, it was automatic and would monitor the heart, also send reports to the doctor's office quarterly. Plus, once a year I go to the doctor's office and have it checked. He asked me if I had any questions. Boy did I ask so many questions he was probably sorry he asked.

The days turned into weeks because of my set back I was going to spend more time than I originally was told. All I wanted now was to get better, so time was on my side!

Just about every day they would send me for all types of test from x-rays to MRI and other types of test, as well as blood work. One of the times they had to take me back to my room because I forgot my pillow. They took x-rays of the defibrillator to be sure the wire was still connected, and everything was working correctly.

After I was done with the lab work, I had to wait for someone to take me back to my room. I be patiently waiting in my wheelchair over a half hour, sometimes even longer. I guess they felt I wasn't going anywhere. It felt like I was in a department store with all the people walking past me.

# "PHYSICAL THERAPY"

My surgeon and his assistant came again to see me a few weeks later which seemed more like months. He asks me how I was feeling. I told him a lot better. He said you are here long enough and was going to release me and suggest I go for physical therapy. His assistant gave me an ID card for the defibrillator so in case I would go through security, I would not be able to go through the X-ray scanner. They both wish me good luck.

One of the administrators came to talk to me about the therapy. She told me she had all the information and would check with my insurance company to get approval. What made it convenient the hospital had its own therapy facility next door.

After a few days I ask them what about the therapy they were still waiting to hear from my insurance company. Now I'm wondering if they will cover the therapy or at least some of it.

Finally, she said I have good news and bad news; "I replied what is the bad news." "Your insurance company declined our request, the good news is, they are looking into a different type of program?"

I was not expecting or prepared to stay longer, so just in case my son Michael purchased some clothing for my extra stay for the therapy.

A few days later I went to rehab, they had approved a seven-day program with an option to extend if needed. It was not as intents as they suggested, but anything would be helpful in my recovery.

I arrived on a Friday I completed the proper paperwork and was weight before going to my assigned room. I was shocked to see my weight was over two hundred pounds. This was the first time I ever weight that much. The nurse told me I most likely am retaining fluids, and once I start therapy the pounds will come off. Plus, they gave me medication to help, another pill to add to my list. They gave me my own personal set of wheels that's a wheelchair to get around in.

Maybe I was spoiled and was expecting the same, but the care was not like the hospital, two nurses took care of a dozen plus patience. It's funny how you learn how to get around the small problems.

I was in a double occupancy room, not like the hospital where I was by myself. When I got to my room,

I noticed that both beds were not made up. The nurse asks me if I had a preface where to bunk. So, I decided to take the bed closest to the front door. Wise choice or not only time will tell?

I finally got my first shower, while I was in the hospital all I got was a wash down with a hot wet soapy sponge. The nurse had to help me undress and shower me than after the shower had to help me dry off and get dress; by this time, it did not even faze me.

I don't think they were too fond of putting on my compression stockings, because I had to remind them almost every time. I laugh now thinking when they put them on it was a job. One of the times the nurse's aide was having a difficult time and slipped and landed on my bed. I laugh and said, "there is only room for one." Finally, after a few attempts she got them on.

They would serve breakfast early, being interrupted during the night I would sleep late. The trouble was when I was ready to eat, I found the breakfast cold. I would hit the call button and of course, it would take a while for someone to come. When I told the nurse about my breakfast, she would scold me and say, "I am not your maid." I would tease her, by saying "but you are." She says, "this is the first and last time no more." She was a real sweetheart and came automatically to heat up my breakfast every morning.

I did not know what to expect, I only remember what they said at the hospital they will be hard on me; oh well time will tell.

I started therapy on Saturday, Sunday was a day of rest. I was just getting used to the fact not having a roommate, no sooner I got one, oh well. He told me his last roommate was a real nuisance and could not get any rest, so he asks for a transfer. In one way it was good to have someone to talk too. But on the other side of the coin he could be a nuisance. I got lucky he was a gentleman with a nice personality. He reminded me of a friend so that made it more enjoyable talking too.

He would complain to the nurses that it was very cold and could feel a draft coming from the window. Now I was glad I pick the bed by the front door. They would raise the thermostat and I would be sweating. It was a no-win situation.

No sooner my new roommate arrived he developed some medical issues and had to go back to the hospital. So, it was back to being alone again.

When I had to go for therapy, an aide would come to my room and help me get into my wheelchair. I would make sure I had my pillow. The aide would take me into this large room. Being it was a Saturday the therapy room was not busy. After my session I was totally out of breath and realize that I needed a lot of therapy if I wanted to get back to somewhat normal.

Came Monday I could not believe the amount of people whom we're getting physical therapy, it seemed a lot were out- patience. It looked like a bus station.

I would receive two sessions a day, one in the morning and another in the afternoon. The nurse was right on the physical therapy part; it was a lot more intense than I anticipated. They had me doing exercises I thought at first, they were trying to kill me. Maybe I was exaggerating, but at that time it felt that way.

They would have me do exercises for half of the session then walk around the room. First, I would walk with assistance, then I was on my own. They said whenever I felt tired just sit down and get back your breath. The problem was it was so crowded I could not find a place to sit even if I wanted too. The hardest part of walking around the room there was so many others doing their therapy it was like being in a traffic jam.

I would see my wheelchair from the other side of the room, and it would look like miles away. That's how exhausted I felt.

They would take my blood pressure and oxygen level serval times during my session.

Each day I was feeling better and getting some of my strength back, but I could feel I still had a long way to go.

With my healing process I had to be careful and have the nurse help me get dress. I tried many times to do it on my own but with no luck.

The afternoon session they would teach me how to get dress, and the proper way to get in and out of bed without putting strain on my upper body; my pillow was always by my bedside and played a big role. Even how to use the bathroom and cleaning yourself. They even showed me the proper way to get in and out of a car and walk up and down stairs. They would have me standing to see how long I could tolerate it. While I was standing, we would play checkers to keep my mind occupied. The first few times I would get tired, but after a while we would play until one of us won.

Believe me, when I say before the therapy there were times, I felt helpless and the therapy really helped. They had these special items to help you get dressed like putting on your socks without bending over and a shoehorn long enough, so you did not have to reach down plus other items for showering.

They would ask me every time I went for therapy the five rules. I had to recite "Cannot pick up more than five pounds, could not put my arms above my head or behind me, could not put any strain on my upper torso, cannot sleep on my belly and had to sit in the back seat of a car." It was like being in school again!

Halfway thru my sessions they requested my insurance company for an extra week of therapy, and it was approved. As much as I wanted to get home, I felt the extra therapy will be to my advantage to a speedier recovery.

During my time at rehab I had to see my surgeon's assistant for a revaluation of my condition. This young aide would wheel me to the hospital to see the doctor and drop me off. Just like any doctor's office I had to wait. After she examined me, said, "everything was healing well, and my weight was coming down." So, it made me feel allot better hearing this. She checks my wrist and remarks it does not look any better than when I saw it last. She cleaned it and put a warm compress over it and said to keep a close eye on it. This seemed to get more attention than my surgery.

She suggested after I finish this program to go for "cardiac therapy; a more intense program, it will do wonders." Again, I had to wait for someone to take me back to my room.

Just about every other day the house doctor would stop by real early like7am and sometimes earlier to check on my progress and make some suggestions. He checks my wrist where I had the swelling and did not like the way it was healing. He put me on a stronger antibiotic, here I'm worrying about my other issue and must encounter another.

I would get into a habit after my afternoon session have them take me to the rec room for a snack. I spend a good half hour and sometimes longer; I do a little reading, chat with other patients. Besides it felt good just to get out of the room. The only drawback was there were times when I wanted to go back to my room there was no one around. They had a bell to ring, but that went on deaf ears. I could not roll myself back because I was told it was too strenuous with my condition. I just had to be patient and eventually, someone would come and roll me back to my room.

I felt bad knowing Marsha was going to celebrate her Birthday in a few days and here I am in rehab. I told my boys let's do a small cake or something. She said, "just get better and we will celebrate when you come home."

They would serve dinner early and I would get hungry about eight; so, I got into this eating habit and hit the call button and just tell them. The nurses or one of the aides would bring me different snacks and coffee. After a couple of times they would bring me snacks on a regular routine. I was getting to enjoy this part of my stay.

I discovered when I went to bed to early, I found myself getting up in the middle of the night. So, I would stay up late, and would sometimes sleep later, except when they came to check my vitals. "What I hated, there was a clock right in view, and I could swear it did not move."

After a few days, I thought I'd be by myself, this one day when I got back from my snack break, I was surprised with a roommate. His name was Mickey and introduce me to his wife Julia, they both seemed very nice. He had a hip replacement and told me that he was having a lot of pain. I tried to help him wherever I could. Everyone had their share of pain or discomfort. I myself was not a fan of any kind of pain medication, even after my surgery I would tolerate the pain. I was taking so much medication I was trying not to add any more to my already long list.

One of the most concerns was getting attention when you needed help; the rehab room service at times was decent but there were times it was just the opposite. The rules required a nurse, or an aid walk you back and forth from the bathroom; their policy was "no one walks alone." I came to discover if you needed assistance to hit the call button at least 15 minutes sooner, sometimes you got lucky and someone came sooner but that was rare.

At the beginning I needed assistance to go back and forth to the bathroom, so I was at their mercy. I once waited over 15 minutes before anyone came. They always had a good excuse, and most likely it was true. There was one time I called, and no one came within a reasonable time, I could no longer wait and walk to the bathroom on my own.

Finally, after a good ten minutes someone comes asking me "who help you." I told the aid "I called over a half-hour ago and could no longer wait." The aid yelled at me for walking on my own. I nicely said, "come at a reasonable time, I don't need an accident." Their remarks were "you are not the only patient."

One night about 3 am my roommate called out to me and ask me to help him out of bed. I asked him if he called for assistance and said, "he could not wait." I felt I was fit to help him, so I came to his rescue; I knew the feeling. I hit the call button It was at least another twenty minutes before somebody finally came. The nurse asks Mickey who help you to the bathroom, and he simply said, "Mike my roommate did, I could not wait." She says to me in a loud tone "you are not strong enough to help others." I wasn't going to argue; I knew my limitations.

Mickey said, "the way they respond to this I don't know what I'm going to do when you leave."

Trying to get some sleep was almost impossible. When they gave me my medication, took blood work and my vitals it was bad enough. Now with a roommate it got that much worse. You would think they would check us the same time.

Now I wonder if I made the right choice picking the bed by the door. Like I said before, "one does not rest in the hospital or here at rehab."

I got to meet many of the other patient's most of them were hip or knee replacements, and they all had a story to tell. It's amazing the kind of people you meet here at rehab.

During my stay they had a meeting with some of the patients and officials from the rehab group. I was invited to attend and express my opinion on my stay. I had no serious complaints except the waiting time for someone to come. They said it was a good argument and they would address the issue.

This other patient kept complaining about almost everything. His biggest concern was he wanted a shower every night at a certain time. The officials tried to explain to him, but it went on deaf ears. We had the same nurses and aides, so I knew he was somewhat exaggerating. He got so annoying I had to say something, it got a little heated up. Then I said, "you must be a lawyer, because you just keep talking and not listening." I hit it on the nail he said "yes, I am."

They had different activities and shows after dinner; it felt good to have a change of scenery. They would come and wheel me from my room and park me so that

I could watch the shows. The entertainment would run about an hour. This one time after one of the shows they must have forgot to wheel me back to my room. I waited patiently, after a half hour I had to shout out to get some attention; finally, someone came for me. They said they did not forget me; I wonder!

Getting company other than my family was not too often especially being so far away from home. I was nicely surprise that two of my fellow workers Terry and Linda payed me a visit. Also, Terry came on a Sunday with her family, they were in the area and that was a nice surprise visit.

One night my roommate Mickey asks me to take a walk with him down to the rec. room. I was always rolled back and forth before. I said okay, he got his walker and I got my pillow and we started walking. By the time we arrived at the rec. room I was tired. It was then I realized how far the micro-wave was when they had to reheat my breakfast. We had some snacks talk awhile and then started back to our room. As much as I thought I was feeling better this only proved I needed more therapy.

One does not realize until you are cooped up how it feels. While I was in rehab my family was down every weekend and it was always good to see them. As time was winding down, they asked me when I was coming home, I told them soon.

Being coop up for over six weeks it was going to feel good going home. For all the time I was in the hospital and rehab I never got to go out and smell the fresh air except when Michael took me outside and that was only for a brief period when it was not cold.  When I was transferred from the hospital to rehab it was an enclosed passageway.

The day before I was being released, they removed the port they had put on me for drawing blood, it hurt more taking it off than putting it on.  After they removed the port it looked like a vampire left his mark.

# "GOING HOME"

Finally, after six long weeks I was being released, the nurse removed my I V and put on a warm compress on my wrist and said, "keep an eye on it".

My son Michael and my wife came to take me home. Originally, he was going to bring his car. I told him to use my car it had much more room, being I had to sit in the back.

I was feeling a lot better but still had a long way to go, to get back to my normal self. I was going to miss some of the people I had gotten friendly with. I went around and thanked all the therapist, nurses and aides for all they had done.

Another chapter closed and moving on to my next program of rehab. I had to make another trip back to the hospital, because my surgeon wanted to see me again for a follow up in about six weeks.

I was on all these new drugs I felt like a druggie. I was scheduled to see my cardiologist in a few weeks, hoping he was going to cut some of my medication. I had lost almost twenty pounds after leaving rehab, I still had some swelling in my legs, so they left me on this special medication until all the swelling went down. It's amazing how one medication can help with a problem but has a side effect and cause other problems. You cannot win!

It felt good to be home, and sleep in my own bed. The first thing I had to do was connect the defibrillator system up. Then take a nice long shower, I had to shower with my back to the water because of the incision. They suggested sitting while showering because of the steam I might get lightheaded and pass out. Something I don't need. While I was in rehab, I ordered a small bench for this purpose, so when I got home it would be there.

Marsha had to put it together, she was able to do it with my supervision. I told her to be sure the screws are tightened. She remarked, "better be nice to me." She had to assist me getting in and out of the shower. It felt so good to be able to shower at home. They were correct at the beginning I did feel a little lightheaded so having the bench was a big asset. As time passed, I was getting to the point where I no longer needed the bench and that made me feel better.

I got used to sleeping on my back, but there were times I almost forgot and realize it when I turn over on to my belly. Like I said my pillow and I were the best of friends. I would hug my heart shape pillow every time I would get in and out of bed.

Normally we would be down at Myrtle Beach for the winter, but because of what happen everything changed. So, we had planned to go after my cardiac rehab, better late than never!

As much as I tried to dress myself, I found it very difficult and Marsha was a big help not to mention everything else, she was doing. I loved the sock helper it made it much easier; even Marsha would use it.

I still had to wear my compression stockings, and the only person that was able to do it was Marsha. When I told her and showed them, she says there is no way I could do it. I assured her we have no choice: watching them do it in the hospital and therapy I explain to Marsha how they did it. We both were surprised when she put them with on with no effort.

Marsha did all the chores that I was doing before my mishap, after a few days I said, "you are going to spoil me." Little by little I was getting more independent on getting dressed. As much as I wanted to do something around the house Marsha, would yell at me every time I tried.

The Monday after I was released a nurse came to check my vitals, she would come twice a week for about three weeks. Then the next day a therapist came to help me with my follow up of my therapy. She asked me questions, like my pass family history and experience with my recent surgery. She gave me some exercises to add to what I was already doing. She had me walk to see what my endurance was. Being it was a mild day we took a walk outside; she reminded me remember we must walk back to the house.

I walked about four minutes and could feel myself starting to get tired, realizing I had to walk back we headed home. When we got back, she explained because I lived on an incline, suggested not to walk straight up but to walk side to side; It made a big difference.

I was always active before this all came about. You do not realize this experience of tiredness and helpless until it happens to you.

Each day I would add an extra minute to my walking, and that seemed to help within a week I was walking ten minutes before getting exhausted. The therapist suggested I go for cardiac rehabilitation after this. I told her this was also suggested by my doctor when I was in rehab.

My local hospital offered this type of therapy. She suggested I call now to make reservation because of the waiting time. She was correct I had to wait two weeks to start.

Now I'm hoping my insurance would cover this, or at least some of the cost. After three weeks of nursing and rehab care they gave me a clean bill of health to continue my recovery.

# "CARDIAC THERAPY"

I went to see my cardiologist, and he examined me and said, "everything was looking good." He suggested making a change on my medications and said that only because one of my medications required going for blood work every week. Not thinking I told him I would stay on it for now.

After four weeks I felt like a pin cushion, it sometimes took the technician two tries and once three times trying to find a vein. With all the bandages I looked like I was wounded.

So, I ask the doctor about another alternative. He told me there is another medication that does not require going for blood work at all. The only reason I did not push it was it was very expensive.

He gave me some free samples and a new prescription for it. When I went to pick it up, I almost had a coronary when the pharmacist told me the going price was five hundred and seventy-five dollars for a thirty-day supply. My doctor was not joking. I guess one cannot put a price on your health.

Just before I was going to start my cardiac rehab my son Michael accompany with my wife went for my follow up visit with my surgeon's assistant. Everything was healing well and got a good report. I also got the okay to drive and suggested just take it easy the first few weeks, so of course I was happy to hear that. Just before we left, she remarks about my hand and said" I see it is healing well."

It was just about lunch time, so we decided to have lunch at the hospital cafeteria. While we were having lunch, I spotted my surgeon having lunch with his assistant whom I had just seen. I had to say hello and thank him again for everything. He at first did not remember, when I told him my name he said, "oh yes you were the lucky one."

I started cardiac rehab not knowing what to expect; I first went for orientation and got a schedule for my sessions. My doctor suggest I go on a thirty-six-session program; three times a week.

After being retired I had no reason to get up early, until now. I would start at 8am and started working out for about forty-five minutes at the beginning and go up to seventy minutes. I was fortunate that I lived just under ten minutes from the hospital. Being retired my time was flexible; many of the other patients, were still employed.

I started out slowly on four different machines. Each week I would do an extra minute and up the level of intensity to my work out. Before and after my exercising session I would do some stretch moves. Then after my work out I would walk around the gym serval times.

I would still do my exercises on the other days at home. I was determined to get back to my normal self no matter the cost.

Each day I could feel myself getting stronger, if I will ever get back to my old self that remains to be seen. First thing, at every session I had to weigh myself before checking in, then I had to attach a heart monitor to my chest. There were many times the nurses had to redo my monitor, because I would miss the spot. You would think by now I have it right.

They would take my blood pressure several times before during and after my exercise session. My first day I thought was rougher than I anticipated; the nurses were very understanding and say work at your own paste.

My cardiologist wanted to get my heart beat up to 110 times a minute. They required a listing of medications I was taking; one of the nurses told me that one of my medications was meant to keep my heart rate down. So, I was fighting an up-hill battle to compete with my medication. So how do I win this battle? There were a few times I got close to my goal, and I could feel the intensity.

They were very health conscience; after using the equipment, we were required to wipe down the machine and equipment with a sterilized disposable cloth.

After my twelve session I was permitted to use the weights, which was easy at the beginning, but as I was getting more into it, I could feel the difference. Halfway thru the sessions I could feel myself getting stronger; what a great feeling.

Beside physical rehab they would have small group meetings on good health habits and how-to relief stress. It is amazing how certain things we do on an ordinary day can cause stress and we do not even realize it. It's hard to change one's routine but after seeing what can cause stress you learn how to get around it the best you can.

A few times I had to cancel my rehab to see my doctors, which only meant it would take that much longer to complete my sessions.

As my time was winding down, they would encourage me as well as everyone else to continue to stay active and get on an exercising program. I was considering different avenues.

We were planning on taking our belated winter get away, just as soon as I finish therapy. I had a few different ideas, I would continue to do my exercises' in Myrtle Beach, and when we got back go to a gym and make it a habit to continue my exercises.

I realize now it's never too late no matter how old one might be. Marsha and I went to check out a health club in our neighborhood and discovered that both our insurance companies covered it totally, so it was a no brainer.

Where does time go, it seems like I just started my therapy. On my last day, they issued me a certificate on my completing the program and wish me good luck. I was going to miss the nurses Thresa, Karen, Michelle, Mary Jane, Nicole, Madelaine and the rest of the crew, and this part of my recovery but that's just another chapter completed in my path to getting back my good health. I continue to do my exercises daily and walk regular and, on my breathing, I was up to 2200ml.

# "IN CLOSING"

We received exciting news that we were expecting another grandchild, and this was like a blessing, which gave me more reason to get back my health so that I could enjoy them and watch them growing up.

I thank God that I can share my experience in writing this. No one knows from day to day what tomorrow might bring. Even though I experience this mishap and the way things happen. I strongly encourage everyone to see their doctors on a regular routine no matter your age, and no matter even if you feel fine.

Remember we are just passing through journey of life; why cut it short. Never be sorry for what you did not due, just what you are going to do. Also, remembering what my surgeon said, "you fell under the 10%, but what about those 90%". So, even if you feel fine one never knows what's happening behind the scenes. What you don't know might save your life; most important think of your family!

Printed in the United States
By Bookmasters